First published in 2018
by GlobalQuest Enterprises
PO Box 89, Warburton VIC 3799, AUSTRALIA

© Keith Simons 2018

This book is copyright. Apart from any fair dealing for the purposes of private study, research or review permitted under the Copyright Act 1968, no part may be stored or reproduced by any process without prior written permission. Enquiries should be made to the publisher.

National Library of Australia
Cataloguing-in-Publication data:

Simons, Keith, 1949-,
Poetica Esoterica/Keith Simons.
ISBN 978-0-9758365-4-51
Simons, Keith, 1949-.

Original hand drawn cover and interior mandalas by
Keith Simons
Cover artwork design by Janet Dado

All true art is a collaboration

4

Prologue

What, my friends, will catch your attention,

What, remove the bored glaze from your eyes,

You, who are suffering tedium,

Who have heard every foolish muttering,

Every esoteric pretence, high and mighty,

Purporting to be truth, wisdom, even proof of divinity,

What can another poet bring to you,

That could possibly be of interest or value,

Are these not more flowery words enticing,

Luring you into worthless webs of meaninglessness,

Slumbering pretentious haughty mumbo jumbo,

Or at best, clever posturing of a wordsmith,

Entertainment with shallowness, as of daily tabloids,

Or is there a slither of an opening, my friends,

A moment: wedge between tedium and interest,

Is there experimentalism, curiosity, intrigue,

Beyond mental certitude that thinks it knows all,
That will allow these words a chance to reveal,
Realms unimagined by weary worldliness,
Vistas suggestive of dimensions wondrous,
That ordinary mind has little inkling of,
Could it be possible that discoveries grand await,
Self-evident inspirations, epiphanies, theophanies?
Can souls awaken to sublime mystical realities?
Could it be that glazed eyes sparkle, shine?
For in truth, forgetfulness is within reach of remembrance,
A mite away from super-sensible consciousness,
A slither from who you really are as eternal souls,
What my friends will inspire you to continue,
To read a prologue intended to spark your interest,
To arouse curiosity, to stimulate, enlighten,
To inspire sufficiently that an epic poem is read?
Read aloud, whether alone or to others,
You may ask, why should I bother?
Find out if you freely choose to, find out!

Hearken

Hearken!
Shining mind of Godhead,

Speaks, exhales, creates,

Painting on blank canvas,

Of infinite space,

Timeless presence,

Speaking one word of harmony,

Original word of loving kindness,

Exhaled into creation's boundless spaces,

Beauty beyond imagination,

Peace beyond comprehension,

Godhead exhales breath,

And creatures move,

In energy spiral webs,

Awaiting embodiments,

Awaiting expanded creativity,

Visioning into space coloured hues,

Layered realities,

Missioning as souls received God-seeds,

Purposing into hearts as hidden treasure,

Flaming sparks of primordial memories,

And then suddenly, forgetfulness,

Suddenly, soul amnesia,

Until!

♦ ♦ ♦

Hearken!

Into great foggy darkness,

I bring light and hope,

A minuscule almost imperceivable,

Penetrating flash,

Lightening stroke, lighting,

Igniting a distant vague feeling,

Heart memory, indescribably sublime,

Soul stirring, potently alive,

For one timeless moment,

All creation dissolved,

Only Creator self aware,

Resting, indwelling, inhaling,

And gradually reflecting,

Deciding!

♦ ♦ ♦

Again hearken!

Deciding, choosing,

To paint new cosmic overlay into being,

Overlay and underlay,

Into-being, into deep memory recesses,

Out into cascading awakenings,

Sparks into flame,

Drops feeding stream,

Word developing lexicon,

Godhead birthing polar contrasting lovers,

But what of multitudes in amnesiac comatose?

What intentional arrow will pierce armour?

Dreamer awaken!

Hearken to these barbed arrows,

Purpose and mission bubbling neath,

Phantasmagoria as a mystery play,

A Lila, play of Godhead,

And then!

• • •

Hearken my beloved,

And then, you can receive arrowed words,

For you are my created masterpiece,

So loved as to be granted freedom,

As I too exercise glorious freedom,

Freedom to soar, to sink, to choose,

To paint on blank canvases of potential,

To exhale into stratospheres,

Into atmospheric earth-bound environs,

Your intentions and imaginings,

To sculpt clay of earthly existence,

Into angelic or demonic shapes,

To create freely as my cosmic agents,

You are my hands,

My eyes and ears,

Your words are mine, on loan,

Your actions, mine, graced by my omnipotence,

Your forgetfulness, mine too,
As a masterwork unrecognised,
Ignored, defiled, corrupted,
Usurped by my own creature,
Awaken, hearken, be at one with me,
Beyond form, within form.

♦ ♦ ♦

What happened in the mists of history,
That beings lost their way,
Became as puppets with blind puppet-masters,
Deaf as deadened, dulled, robots,
Chasing shadows as if they had substance,
Lusting for mirages that evaporate in despair,
Projecting enemies from inner delusion,
What happened to Gods children?
Is freedom a curse after-all,
Is physical embodiment a prison to be endured?
Has Godhead abandoned us,
Hearken! I'll tell you true,
It is impossible for me to abandon you,

Can parents abandon their children?

Alas, it is you who have abandoned me.

◆ ◆ ◆

Hearken!

Freedom is a stranger in a strange land,

There is no unchanging stability here,

No security of knowing when death will visit,

No relying on nature's consistency,

Freedom is unpredictable,

It pounces when least expected,

Shatters and reinvigorates,

Flatters and disintegrates,

And yet, without freedom you would be unlike me,

In my glory,

In my innermost being-ness,

My face with a thousand expressions,

Personality with multiple facades,

Mind with uncountable thoughts,

Without freedom the cosmos would have no narrator,

No play of consciousness,

No conscience, nor opportunity for redemption,

But with freedom shadows lurk too,

For they too were born of my greatest gift.

♦ ♦ ♦

Hearken my children!

It was secretly planted within the very soul of creatures,

That treasures lost could be found again,

And with no losing there would be no joy of finding.

With no going astray, no joy of finding the way,

And with no submerging into dark underworlds,

No lighting those dank, putrid places,

Without contrast you would never know joy,

This, paradox is a blessing.

A blessing wearing many disguises,

Here freedom frolics and evolves,

Here once upon a time, countless moons ago,

Freedom birthed anew despite dire warnings,

So myths of old inform,

Echoes from far distant ancestral lineages,

Recalling a choice with awesome consequences.

♦ ♦ ♦

Hearken, listen closely to this epic tale,

It is where your beginnings yet whisper,

Reminding of freedom once chosen,

When Godhead released nature to another fate,

When Demi-Gods ruled kingdoms,

Powers greater than nature herself,

Powers that could flourish or destroy,

For now the sword of Damocles hung over creation,

Mighty Zeus ruled with Hera by his side,

But now joined by a pantheon of Goddesses and Gods,

Representing autonomous forces,

All loosed upon cosmic and worldly history,

Even down to this very day,

This very omnipresent, eternal moment,

Each passing moment with its gifted freedom,

Wrought in a crucible of momentous choice,

And yet, no real choice at all,

Adam had been seduced by inner longing.

Voices of fear rise up, and warn him,

Do not be seduced by the asp of unknown desires,

That would grant you freedoms beyond nature,

Grant you promises of independence,

Voices of dire consequences hiss and splutter,

You will be beyond nature, free of her rulership,

You will no longer be obliged to adhere naturally,

As other creatures do with blind obedience,

As tempests, volcanos, earthquakes obey me,

You will forget who you are,

Moving freely hither and thither,

Across territories vast, and oceans wide,

You will think it your privilege to conquer nature,

And pillage your mother, reduce her to a whore,

For your whims and insatiable power-lust,

So it was, that voices of prophetic fear sounded forth,

But they could not prevent a greater power,

That issued from Godhead's own vision,

To choose freedom above all other considerations.

◆ ◆ ◆

Hearken, do not cower,

Nor cover your ears, trembling, quavering,

For price paid for freedom,

Is your most glorious hope, and more-so,

Your sacred duty and innermost mission,

Hidden behind misty clouds of forgetfulness,

It is what it always has been,

Godhead's ultimate purpose for creating your universe,

For initiating souls into whirlpools of freedom,

Beginning with one almighty choice,

To release some creatures from instinct,

And infuse them with self-reflection,

As in a mirror, even if somewhat darkly,

To infuse them with autonomy,

Even if mixed with nature's own branding,

To empower tongues with speech,

Beyond nature's own bounty,

And below what is easily perceived,

Gently guide humanity towards Paradise,

Envisioned in depths beyond surface thinkings,

Beyond mundane pursuits,

Depths of soul-potential that await,

An awakening like no other,

When heaven and earth embrace,

In celebration destined by design,

Within Godhead's original intention,

And yet for now, a question looms,

What will further this epic tale,

To liberating quantum strides,

Towards fulfilling your own soul's secret vision!

♦ ♦ ♦

Hearken, dear friends,

Together we forge a new epoch,

Clustered in mutual endeavours,

Even whilst separation swings,

This way and that, unison brings,

Loveliest appreciations of nature's common-wealth,

Restoring empathy and sublime connection,

And remembrance of a sacred pact,

Made at the dawn of history,

To be as loving caretakers and friends,
Companions to all living others,
Who in truth are our sisters and brothers,
That this heart revelation breaks asunder,
Generations of separation and narcissism,
Deconstructs eons of intellectual pride,
Resurrects soul-yearning for authentic relationships,
Revolutionises consciousness in blazes of inspired gnosis,
Invigorates world weary souls with divine nectar,
Sacrifices burdens carried in dazed stupor,
Immediately, a lighter step,
A gait bespeaking of transformation's magic,
A motioned posture beautiful to observe,
Art regaining its highest calling,
All this and more, replacing dying ghosts,
Will further this epic tale, true and good.

◆ ◆ ◆

My dear friends, hearken anew,
Good news is upon us,

Light penetrates through cracks in underworld caverns,
Mephistopheles cannot ignore my shafts,
We wrestle in pools and lakes,
Splashing about in frenzied combat,
Thrashing, resisting, screaming obscenities,
But my friends, to no avail is this rear-guard action,
For once light beams have entered dark citadels,
Time itself befriends Godhead's servants,
Here then is good news for those who have ears to hear,
Together we hearken!
Allowing gold tipped arrows to pierce our hearts,
Change is activated this very moment,
Change begins within our hearts and minds,
Within and then after incubation, without,
Without, in spirals of unforced grace,
As heartfelt outpourings of angelic beauty,
As reaching out towards each other,
In soul-connectivity, joyful smiles,
Together and alone we weave along.

In solitude and companionship we sing our song,

Transcending gravitational pull of Lucifer's desires,

Rising above his outdated fires,

Witnessing drama heaped upon drama,

From eagle's lofty vantage,

Subtly nodding our pledge to the great work,

Of incarnating Godhead's vision into earthly domain,

Knowing we too are constructed of stardust,

Of stellar light, that is God's own body,

That father and son,

Mother and daughter, are unified eternally,

And even Mephisto will be transfigured by love,

Even Lucifer will turn towards love of Godhead,

All this happening within each of us every heart-beat,

As we forge our way-journeys inspired by light,

Towards greater light into supernal brilliance,

Here a glimpse to help soul travellers aright.

♦ ♦ ♦

Hearken, do not ignore signs,

Messages from nature's kingdom,

Nature is God's intermediary,

Her language, of portents, guidances,

When intelligence is deaf and blind,

When humble reverence is dull and insipid,

And nature rears up in extreme agitation,

It's pained response dreadful indeed,

Arrogance will not withstand her fury,

It will be washed away in torrents of tears,

And yet if this is a way to awaken the beloved,

It must be so,

It must be nature's own contribution to our epic tale,

Even as hordes will be unprepared,

Staring in shocked awe at unleashed spectacles,

Nature in this manner will restore balance,

And present day ancestors of mythic Noah,

Will float on high seas of destiny,

Will ride out the furious storm,

Until a freshly washed land offers new beginnings,

Amidst devastation and wailing,

Souls in greater numbers will reconstruct from ruins,

Here my friends, is hope engendered by Godhead's vision,

Moreover, purpose and mission, buried deep,

Awaiting kiss of life giving abundance.

♦ ♦ ♦

Hearken my long suffering friends,

A disease incrementally creeps, crawls,

Seeps into every crevice and crack,

As light does, blending, admixing, conjoining,

Together, demons dance with angels,

In a two-step, destined to climb to a summit,

An apex, that thunders and roars,

Where entangled dancers suffocate,

A moment that typifies breakthrough or breakdown,

For this dance of contrasting styles,

Can only reconcile in radical transformed relationship,

As this relationship remains unhealed, in limbo,

Disease slowly calls death ever nearer,

Death too is a wake up call,

Crossing over a threshold into remorse,

For wasting this precious human embodiment,

For allowing angels to co-habit with demons,

And if we can learn a lesson whilst incarnated,

What might that be dear ones,

That any moment a commitment is made,

Towards union with Godhead,

To devotional supplication, with hands folded,

With heart and mind yoked in loving service,

Would not such a moment be a wondrous turning,

A joyful act of renunciation,

A yes vote for holistic integration and harmony,

A new dance welcoming a future yet to fully manifest,

Be then aware of Mephisto's cunning schemes,

Appealing to voids unfilled by creative living,

Seductively enticing lost souls into sensory traps,

Gilded cages manufactured to enslave,

Beware of cunning adversary within too,

Ingrained chaser after phantoms,

They will target your weaknesses,

Hook you into empty promises,

Lured into caverns of outrageous sensuality,

Entice you to experiment wildly without restraint,

And dear souls, all this must be acknowledged,

For materialism knows no bounds,

And yet, it is possible to turn about,

To overcome, overwhelm, transfigure,

It has always been free choice,

Freedom's ultimate move.

♦ ♦ ♦

It's been a long struggle,

As cosmic evolution passed through its spiralling movement,

Hearken therefore, as this ode invites a plunge,

Submergence into dark places,

But with a lamp to light the way,

A plunge, not to be entrapped nor seduced,

Rather to meet Mephisto with a soulful 'no',

For only then will he retreat,

And again and again,

Soul stands firm and says 'no',

No to his temptations and glue-like offerings,

No to all that soul knows to be false and shallow,

In this manner, reminiscent of a dying witch,

Who in truth was already dead,

Mephisto can die too and be reborn as friend,

A friend who will serve all life,

As servant of the most high,

Eventually eon-long struggle will give way,

Dissipate, dissolve into etheric mists,

As cosmic recycling continues without your personal anguish,

At what momentous moment will you step into your glory,

Once and for all,

Or are you enmeshed in a struggle between forces!

♦ ♦ ♦

Hearken! Honesty enters and must speak,

Who can say, my struggle is over,

Who can utter silken words, such as,

'As molten lava running down mountainside,

Yes, I am such a one who has fully pledged,

Fully sacrificed and renunciated,'

Certainly not most human-kind,

And here we come upon a bridge,

That indeed you are crossing but haven't crossed,

That you are living yet only with dimmed light,

Honesty proclaims with compassionate empathy,

Bridge builders you may be,

And bridge crossers your destinies,

But for now, as cocoons between caterpillar and butterfly,

Be at peace with struggle,

Understand incrementalism as a slow love affair,

Bridging as it must, one step at a time,

Depending where on the bridge you are,

Meditate my dear friends on this timeless theme,

This coupling of dimensions,

Twin threads in a complex tapestry,

Both bridge builder and bridge crosser,

Both bridegroom and bride,

And you will span the girth.

♦ ♦ ♦

Always hearken!

For inattention invites invisible demons,

They are parasites imitating your thoughts,

Hiding in cloudy realms,

Waiting for openings, opportunities,

To infiltrate and take up residence,

In physical hosts as humans are,

Always hearken dear friends,

For demonic longing for sensuality,

Encased in flesh and warm blood,

Is insatiably food for hungry ghosts,

Hence I have insisted that 'will' must be strong,

Stronger than thought and emotion,

Will is action deriving from soul,

Soul is a hand-servant of Spirit,

Spirit is Godhead,

Godhead is Spirit is Soul is Will,

And my dear friends, will is grace in action,

Therefore overcome addictive enslavement,

To the voices of demonic desire and power-lust,

And be as angels in human form.

♦ ♦ ♦

Hearken! Cosmic storm waters are flushing through your land,

Dreams crumbling into ashen grave yards,

Greed is piling misery atop of its own demise,

Heeding not these warnings only postpones,

Only holds back inevitable outcomes,

From all quarters nature's voice resounds,

Your matricide is not sanctioned by Godhead,

Your ecoside is abhorrent to Spirit,

Raping Mother Earth is suicidal,

You cut your own life giving artery,

So awaken now and turn your face to the sun,

Embolden will and renounce greed,

Be born again, aligned to cosmic parents,

Alchemically transform storm waters into baptisms,

Rejoice in crucified rebirth, live anew,

Your heart can burn with passion fires,
Your mind with enthusiasm and creative ardour,
Will can be as a winged chariot, bringing hope and joy,
Hope to the hopeless, joy to the joyless,
And love to those who know only hate and revenge,
Begin now, with an inner pledge, and err no more.

♦ ♦ ♦

Hearken, listen to your own soul,
Banish Mephisto from your heart and mind,
Your soul has treasures buried within,
Within vaults of your heart chambers,
And here one secret chamber is a portal to Godhead,
This chamber contains soul's innermost voice of conscience,
It alone knows right from wrong,
It knows freedom's movement as sacred wayfarer,
This treasure chest once opened cannot be closed,
Consciousness has undergone a forever shift,
Pandora's box-lid has been wrested open,
And all sprites, loving and evil alike,

Have escaped the dark underworld of unconsciousness,

To now be seen in broad daylight,

For my dear friends, this is reckoning true,

True judgement without blame,

Alchemical crucible broiling with active redemption,

An incubative transformation that will birth a butterfly.

♦ ♦ ♦

Read these words aloud to your soul,

It is a testament we share as kith and kin,

Hearken together, shedding tears of remorse,

These stanzas are healing balms,

From beloved friends, extended soul family,

Gifting you as loving parents are impelled to do,

With shock waves and gentle ripples both,

To awaken, remind, plant fresh seeds,

To toil your tired soil into robust living earth,

To refresh your heart so joy can enter,

My mission then can align with your own,

As the March of evolution refines, refocuses,

As Shambala descends from etheric realms,
Manifesting as a garden of beauty,
A manifested physical representation of Godhead's vision,
Indeed, our very own soul's innermost vision,
So read these words aloud as ambrosia for your soul,
Listen to these gifted words as from your own soul,
For my friends, we are one in spirit,
We are one, all one, united in spirit,
Separated as fingers are and yet part of one hand,
And together a benediction is upon us,
As we share these soul inspired words,
As one inter-connected inter-being Spirit Self,
Homo-Spiritus!

Hallelujah

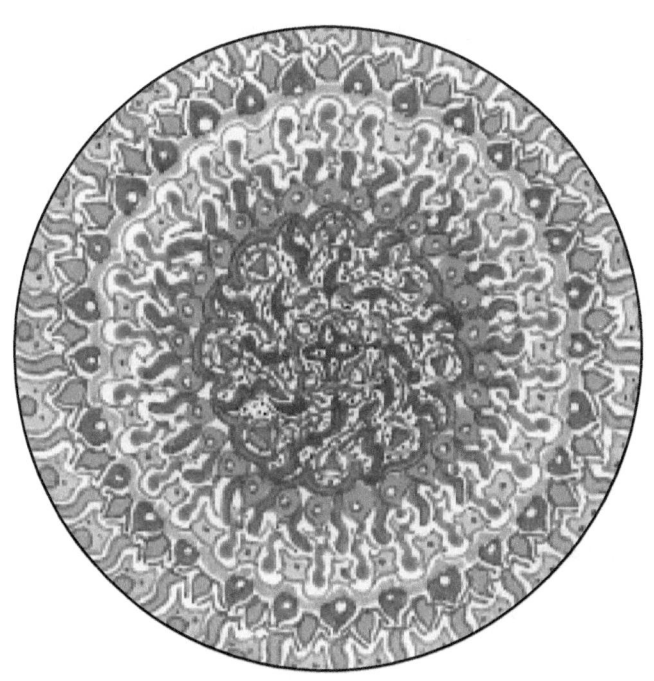

New life begins at any moment chosen,

First shafts of dawn's light,

First independent breath of a newborn,

Introduced with shades of humour,

A twinkle in an unseen eye,

To lighten mood and invite inner smile,

To engage heart with childlike hope,

Piercing clouds into etheric radiance,

Raising mind to inspirational heights,

Birthing anew, from death's released grip,

A super-nova reconstituted,

From pre-used star dust,

A cosmic event replicated here on earth,

An alchemical transmutation before our eyes,

Even as cells, persons and communities,

Evolve and strive towards secret dreams,

Even as heart-connected soul clusters,

Discover synergy in coherent movements,

As sunlight breaks through clouds,

As birds flying in beatific unison,

As scribes sharing divinely inspired words!

New life is chosen,

Hallelujah!

♦ ♦ ♦

Hope embedded in heart's secret cove,

Secretly seeking for its beloved,

This search has origins in antiquity,

In separations that set this epic in motion,

When hearts became divided,

When eyes became dual, ears likewise,

Polarities emerged and began seeking,

Seeking for their other half,

Symbiotic twins apart with different faces,

Trillions of different forms,

Spreading out across the universe,

Across your garden planet in astonishing variety,

And when two souls merge in loving embrace,
When duality melts into transcendent unity,
When energy fields replace atomic apartness,
Then bliss filled reunions rejoice,
Gulfs between lovers evaporate like morning mists,
Whence if you listen carefully, you will hear,
Hallelujah!

♦ ♦ ♦

Humanity, entangled in self-made mesh,
Woven by myriads of karmic weavings,
Myriads beyond number of momentary choices,
Clever, sophisticated but unintelligent,
Ingenious, skilful but inhumane,
Desiring more whilst shrivelling,
Expressing more yet drivelling,
Denying, escaping, deluding,
Until as in fairy tales oft told,
An awakening suddenly occurs,
Saving grace untangles, unfurls,
A cloth of a thousand threads,

Enters into another seamstress's hands,

And with dexterity born of sincere devotion,

Old rags become transformed,

Transformed into objects beautiful,

New clothes for old,

Humanity reformed, emerging from underworlds,

Breaking free of incubative cocoons,

This my dear friends, awaits you,

Hallelujah!

♦ ♦ ♦

You incarnated to contribute dear friends,

To collective endeavours,

Inspiring each other with stories shared,

Spurring each other to greater deeds,

Joining together in mutual enthusiasm,

Mutual creative initiatives,

Breaking free from societal apathy,

And soul-destroying blind conformity,

Turn about and observe another road,

Notice special sign-posts pointing,

Pointers to tomorrow's destiny,

Here, the edge on which you dwell,

Pulled and pushed, twixt life and death,

Choosing life, always choosing life,

Breaking out from history's stranglehold,

With its manipulations, indoctrinations,

Freedom choosing a finer destiny,

Choosing love, kindness, creative contributions,

Joining with others collaboratively,

Building new worlds, together,

Hallelujah!

◆ ◆ ◆

Struggle is preferable to unchanging stasis,

A seed ought not stay buried forever,

It should break through earthly crust,

A fragile sprig, watered and warmed,

Becoming sapling, nature's childhood,

And so on towards maturity,

Nature's adolescence and adulthood,

Is this not nature's metamorphic struggle?

And from adulthood decaying seeds are blown,

Seeds once again are sown,

For life-intelligence spirals incessantly,

Ever out-stripping previous forms,

Reaching for ideals bubbling into existence,

Bursting, cascading from latency to actuality,

Or quietly seeping almost unnoticed,

And yet, my dear friends,

Understand well such metaphors,

For they bespeak of your own soul-growth,

Your own spiralling motion,

Within the core of sacred being-ness,

Consciousness becoming self-aware,

I am that I am, no longer of Godhead alone,

Now homo-spiritus in self cognisant freedom,

In meditative at-one-ness beyond division,

In divine contemplation of one behind many,

One within many, permeating, penetrating,

One field, one glorious divine breath,

One consciousness expressing through billions of minds,

And as this epiphany explodes across humanity,

As a collective awakening, a tidal wave,

Washing ignorance and self-forgetting into channels,

Far from destiny's loadstar and beckoning,

Struggle itself will be gratefully thanked,

For has it not led to the promised land,

This vision exists deep within our souls,

We shall turn to face one another, and joyfully,

Sing Hallelujah!

♦ ♦ ♦

Do not spurn utopian visions,

The great adversary would have you believe,

That utopias are deluded imaginations,

Devoid of any worthy considerations,

Fantasies of childish desperation,

Fairy tales intended for immature sprites,

But I tell you what your heart already knows,

Utopia is closer than cleverness can reveal,

Do you not see in illuminating flashes of revelation,

How adversary both without and within,

Has duped you, befuddled you with nonsense,
Twisted native intelligence into fearful concepts,
Tangled minds into layered hubris,
That in truth only showcases intellectual stupidity,
Can you not awaken this very moment,
And discard Mephisto's insidious taunting,
His devilish mental and emotional gymnastics,
And turn to your soul's simple yet sublime wisdom,
Wisdom will immediately open a gateway,
A sacred gateway into a utopia that exists,
Pulsates, beckons, awaits recognition,
It is closer than your heart-beat,
And at that moment of soul epiphany,
You will exclaim in celebration with me,
Hallelujah!

♦ ♦ ♦

Demonic forces should never be under-estimated,
Those obstacles that thwart, divert, distort,
Utopia so close and so far,
As demons tempt with every wile,

Every craftiness and lustfulness,
With blood thirsty appetites,
Appealing to senses undisciplined,
Gluttonous, intoxicated, bewitched by phantoms,
Forms appearing desirous to raging hunger,
Driven almost mad with carnal cravings,
Grasping with outstretched hands,
Bulging eyes, tongues snake-like,
Nostrils flared in sensual aromatic haze,
Disembodied souls, ghouls, hungry ghosts,
Parasitically inhabiting, usurping, demanding,
My friends, do not under-estimate these demons,
Nor think they do not hover in close proximity,
Waiting for human weaknesses to open gates,
Openings inviting demons, giving licence,
Freedom to indulge and rule,
Until fateful vital inner soul voice,
Overwhelms these forces of sensual desire,
These compensatory, empty, futile longings,
Over powers these forces of rampant materialism,

These insatiable bony fingers of greed and need,

When soul regains and sits on its rightful throne,

Atop of mountain, witnessing all folly below,

In the valley of discontent,

And my dear fellow soul travellers,

When atop of that spirit mountain you have rested,

And strengthened in moral fibre,

You may choose to descend again into lowlands,

With teachings inspired by fires of inner alchemy,

Hallelujah!

◆ ◆ ◆

So you should now see more clearly,

How this epic poem mirrors life itself,

It should be lucidly obvious,

How human incarnation offers blessings,

That must be earn't by sacrifice,

By freely chosen renunciation,

By inspired choices that open sacred pathways,

And many other cultivations, reparations,

Many refinements, polishing a diamond,

Encrusted with layers of evolutional mud,

For the soul-diamond that sleeps and dreams,

Also dreams of waking, remaking,

Recalibrating, and renouncing,

This, thorny passage we must all traverse,

If your epic journey is to deliver you home,

From whence we originally departed,

On an adventure too magnanimous for limited words,

That even a glimpse can embolden and propel,

Souls to deeds of spirit wealth,

Deeds that find echoes of rejoicing,

In all worlds, all dimensions, all cosmos,

Issuing forth a sound-wave, that inner ear can hear,

A sound vibrating and resonating throughout time-space,

A celebratory word,

Hallelujah!

♦ ♦ ♦

Stanza's will come and go, appear and be gone,

As existence pulsates in and out,

Forming, transforming and disappearing,
All that can be created can be destroyed,
And yet hidden within this whirling matrix,
An eye watches in mystic constancy,
An ear hears with unbroken consistency,
An eternal over-self witnesses,
As stanza's appear and vanish,
Universes likewise pulse into existence,
And are swallowed again into emptiness,
But my dear friends, a secret is here revealed,
That no matter how many stanza's and universes,
Vanish from sight, consumed by emptiness,
Another will emerge, and bring into new forms,
Essences derived from all that once was,
You are carriers of distant knowledge,
Repositories and holy servants,
You are safe guarders of cosmic treasures,
Unbeknown to your ordinary mind,
But felt within sacred heart chambers,
You are Godhead's missionaries in dreamland,

You can awaken this very moment,

Realising that where a dream is, so is a dreamer,

Where a thought, so a thinker,

Where a universe, a witness who created it,

You are in thought and in deed, a co-creator,

As again we intone our gratitude,

Hallelujah!

Freedom

Every soul, intimate representative of humanity,

Biography of one, can describe many!

A soul inhabiting a tiny body,

Unable yet to walk or talk,

With inner eye open wide,

With faculties beyond intellect's range,

A being come again from infinity,

Re-entered once again, mortal coil,

Knowing more than minds abounding,

A mystery unfolding in limbs and organs,

In flesh and bones, heart and mind,

A being as yet in infant casing,

For a while in paradise, translucent, shimmering,

For another entry into an epic mystery play,

Bringing soul gifts from invisible spaces,

Such a soul wrapped in baby's blankets,

Huddled in protective swaddling,

And a dream was dreamt about this phase,

A dream that all was safe, utopian bound,

As a boat floating on calm ocean waters,

With divine parents aboard in trust and love,

Nothing to perturb soul in watery heaven,

Until innocence is forever shifted,

Paradise lost begins its share,

A stormy sea with turbulence, thunder,

Parents revealed as imperfect,

Not God and Goddess to be trusted pure,

But human all too human in danger's hold,

The soul encased in a tiny body,

Is welcomed into dream world's struggle,

A rite of passage, first of many,

As soul imbibes drama unfolding,

Growth by loss of innocence pending,

This the way of incarnation,

Another round of initiations,

Chosen in freedom!

✦ ✦ ✦

T'was this first dream that set a tone,

Of shock waves alerting, alarming,

Fight or flight from distant past,

Re-visiting as raw emotion,

Here, genesis of nightmares,

Scenes terrifying, caught in cellular memory,

Re-activated, filtered into eternal now,

Images so real, small body trembles,

Stormy seas with sharks circling,

Father sliding into surging waters,

Desperately clinging, youngster watching helplessly,

Then shifting, another dream-scape,

Scenes become double edged,

Soul watching itself apart,

Split into self and other, both as two,

One part as in mirror reflection,

One that is real and true,

Here dear friends, humanities departure,

From paradise's harmony and unified field,

A story with duplicity, conflict,

A complex dream so strange, bizarre,

For soul is both inside and out,

Centre of gravity moving about,

Child by now is waveringly, walking,

Mouthing words, a common few well known,

Soon enough the world will enter,

A waking dream, complex and scary,

With rules numerous insisted by,

Authorities looming large, in school yards,

And yet these episodes that we all endure,

That in truth are hidden behind externalities,

Are chosen in freedom!

♦ ♦ ♦

Here a retracing of cosmic development,

Replicating, imitating, in its fashion,

On ground of human striving forth,

Another spiral twist and turn,

As dreams take up chosen contents, from past,

As with ingredients that endure, long last,

Reconstituting them into fresh patterns,

As childhood merges into adolescence,

With primal urges now unleashed,

Hormones themselves awaken, erupt,

Intense passions aroused, occasionally exploding,

Obsessive themes occupy, insistent,

Tendencies attached often re-loading,

Soul could fly if it grew wings,

It could die for the beloved,

Or live eternally for her,

In blissful abandon,

Sophia would take hold of soul,

Capture it in wildest perception,

Projected upon gendered love-twin,

Vision of beauty that eyes can barely behold,

That heart alone can withstand in dazzlement,

An experience of divinely enraptured love,

Accompanied by another dream,

Of two perfect lovers walking hand in hand,

Away from all that would imprison them,

Into an unknown, yet heart known future,

A choice made in freedom!

♦ ♦ ♦

Alongside sublime beauty, shadows lurk,

Counter-force of frustrated passion,

Where supernal dream and mortal reality clash,

In and out do not move in natural sympathy,

Cultural norms intersect, block and blur,

Here again splitting, fragments occur,

Internal voices diverging, confusing,

Fantasies forming in revolt, refusing,

And double-self incarnates as secret companion,

This epic saga now complicating, bemusing,

No longer parts harmoniously fusing.

As multiple characters dwell within singularity,

Multiplicity reigns and agitated duplicity,

All portions vying for rulership,

To fulfil their varied agendas,

No peace reigns in this fractured palace,

This temple in disarray, tortured with malice,

Here overlaid by masks and lies,

Are soul traumas, stories untold,

Fractured wholeness, must now unfold,

Here an opening for myriads of therapeutic inroads,

Doctors of the soul in guises of every type,

Of every quality and self-healed actuality,

And my dear friends, it is so,

That you will experiment with, be attracted to,

Those that resonate with your inner trajectory,

Creating gradually a healthier inventory,

Your orientation gradually wrought in a living crucible,

Of choices freely made!

♦ ♦ ♦

How free are choices, you may ask,

If for instance demons rule,

Or even if angels guide,

Might they be imposters cruel,

Does that suggest freedom won,

Or another form of enslaved tyranny,

Where does freedom enter in,

Amidst this complex, varied din,

I'll tell you in simple terms,

That freedom sits betwixt these forces,

Truly, there exist numerous courses,

It is exactly your capacity to chose,

Despite habitual preferences strengthened,

By countless, innumerable past choices made,

That substantially imprinted, a life inlaid,

All with a degree of chosen freedom,

Incrementally weaving in intricate flow-forms,

Inter-weaving, yet with free choice involved,

Establishing ever changing, shifting norms,

As soul has within its sphere,

A power greater than nature's own,

A power of choosing freely, your own renown,

Of choices made in freedom!

♦ ♦ ♦

Maturity of soul is hard won indeed,

Not gained by surface fancies,

Nor by clever pretence or acting skills,

Maturity is a ripened tree,

Not a sapling, nor branch,

But rather a whole tree thriving,

Bearing fruit, providing nourishment,

A mature soul has ripened so,

Through free choices that helped it grow,

And dear friends, be at peace,

Knowing that every choice made by you,

That is Spirit guided, pure and true,

Every tiny choice or huge,

Reforms, recreates, moves towards your bliss,

Towards tomorrow's spirit kiss,

No free choice with spirit's stamp,

Should be perceived with fogged disdain,

For each moment of finer choices,

Builds maturity in its stead,

Each moment graced by soul awakened,

Inspires choices made in freedom!

♦ ♦ ♦

It was in adolescence then,

When another divide occurred,

A schism between two parts,

Twin selves, co-habituating,

In inner discord, one judging the other,

In perpetual uncomfortableness,

A tale here essentially common,

Yet individually unique in detail,

In composition, in complexity,

This furthering and deepening of conflicted self,

Triggered by one event or another,

A catalyst set another layer in motion,

Another layer of secrecy and shame,

As symbiotic play moved into shape,

And another dream revealed clearly,

Three parts, a development from duality,

A trinity now, with an overseer commentating,

As two parts swung like a pendulum,

Being often too much or too little,

Inflated or deflated, undisciplined or overly austere,

A trinity now that would accompany soul life,

Into and through years,

Years spanning a wide spectrum of experience,

Joys, miseries, easy-rides, difficult challenges,

With varying degrees of resolution and balance,

But gradually maturing in insight,

As choices continued to be made in freedom!

♦ ♦ ♦

Now in the twilight of incarnated life,

With ageing body, aching limbs,

What lessons have been learnt,

Worthy of the telling,

More-so, justifying an epic ode,

What wisdom can be possibly passed on,

That could possibly make a difference to you, dear soul,

For perfection in this human realm,

Is impossible to achieve,

Except within innermost soul,

Tell me this, what does not die?

Only the deathless can achieve perfection,

Tell me this too, what in you is deathless?

I will share something, hearken!

A soul's attachments prevent peace,

Attachments cause suffering,

Even being attached to non-attachment brings anxiety,

They expel souls from paradise,

Remove them from still waters,

From the power of now,

Attachments rob souls of flexibility,

And most alarmingly of all,

They shake them loose from freedom,

Glue consciousness to objects,

Narrow view into tunnels,

And yet from a wider view,

It can be understood that freedom,

Always chooses it's own imprisonment.

This then I share with you,

That free choice is always present,

In everything we do and don't,

That behind the human drama,

Ever changing in its play,

Seemingly handing out fortune and misfortune,

Randomly without rhyme or reason,

Freedom of choice is active too,

And yes, consequences are often predictable,

In ways that appear determined fast,

Unmovable as if thus victimised,

But all has fingerprints of choices made,

And my friends here is hope,

For free choice can future bring,

Changed fortunes in their wake,

And here too wisdom learnt,

That each choice has merit great,

Beyond immediate observation,

For consequences are like winding roads,

Only seeing to the closest bend,

Or horizons that extend beyond your view,

So imperfect as finite is,

Infinity sits behind in silence,

As imperfect as time must be,

Eternity is without flaw,

In transcendent meditative being,

You too can touch infinity and eternity,

For it is the ground of your being,

From which freedom of choice is granted!

♦ ♦ ♦

Each moment choices being made,

Under conscious radar mostly,

Whispers from other realms, ghostly,

Multitudes of moment by moment choices,

Incrementally adding and subtracting,

Strengthening and weakening,

Forces that account for everything,

Everything, known as you and yours,

Suggestive voices prompting chores,

Be aware, how freedom of choice,

Is vulnerable to varied a voice,

Makes merry or sad, not randomly so,

Brings forth laughter or tears that flow,

Choices driven by others, past done,

That now colour mood, misery or fun,

To whatever degree gifted freedom alive,

A breeze or gale that aids soul to strive,

Every moment of every hour, without fault,

Every day of every year, without halt,

And every incarnation across the universe,

A continuum, life's creative stream,

Eternally shaping and re-shaping.

Within inter-woven networks of relationship,

Inter-dimensionally, always inter-connectively,

A gigantic web wherein momentary choices,

Influencing cosmic dramas abounding.

Within intaking and out sounding,

Influencing cosmos every moment,

And yet may feel as in dream states,

That self is powerless and impotent,

Asking what is value of life itself,

What the point, is all not in vain,

In response I tell true and plain,

Cosmos is also self, as destiny's quiet impulse,

Do we listen, or does deafness prevail,

Are we guided, or do we fail,

And of most significance, my dear friends,

Are potent destiny moments,

Choices made in freedom that impact greatly,

On your forever changing life biography,

Inherent, sacred, freedom of choice!

♦ ♦ ♦

'Tis this epic saga inherited jointly,

With hidden impulses sounding forth,

A musician knowing not from where sounds emanate,

Self knowing not one's true identity,

A finger believing it has autonomous existence,

Believing a hand is superstitious imagining,

That body is mythic nonsense,

Self reduced to mental conceptualism,

Reduced, shrivelled into arrogant pride,

Hubris maintained by rigid make-belief,

Where ego equates to forgetfulness,

And yet dear friends,

Hidden impulses are likewise benedictions,

Blessings merely awaiting shafts of remembrance,

A striking bolt of conscious re-cognition,

Sudden sacrificing of indoctrinations,
Releasing grip of phantoms grasping,
Entering into mysteries beyond concept's masking,
Knowing nought, yet knowing truth,
Impulses pulsating in cosmic existence,
Omni-presently within and everywhere without,
That would alchemically recalibrate,
Every cell, reinvigorate, within Godhead's play-field,
If only soul would open a gate,
That could revolutionise a human fate,
And the secret of secrets astounding here,
Is that free choice can make it so,
If that is where you choose to go!

♦ ♦ ♦

Hence freedom is hydra indeed,
Two headed creature, two mouths to feed,
Freedom choosing as food provider,
What mouth to feed, what head to heed,
And if human nature is dual this way,
Can reconciliation become a re-birthed day,

A day when sun and moon dance,

In harmonic unison without blemish,

When the human family become truly one,

When all living creatures are loved,

For simply being what they are,

Treated as Godhead's children all,

When earth garden regains its perceived sacredness,

Children are seen as reincarnated souls,

With mystical impulses expressed as goals,

When one's own unique gifts are brought out,

Shared as contributions to Godhead's mission,

Indeed what head do we focus upon,

What mouth do we give our attention to,

Moment by moment, building into hours,

Hour upon hour, day into day,

Incarnated embodiments countless in number,

Forming, reforming, transforming,

With every moment influencing this parade,

With freedom of choice, at its very core.

◆ ◆ ◆

Freedom is key and keystone,
To understand, deeply comprehend,
Intuitively penetrate into cosmic mystery,
Into Godhead's mind and intention,
Into chorus mystica, music of the spheres,
Freedom is Godliness in human incarnation,
When aligned with divine source,
By incarnating into fleshly bodies,
With amazingly sophisticated brains,
Movable limbs, complex nerves and organs,
All replicating cosmic complexity,
A microcosm is funnelled into existence,
From cosmic perspective, a microbe,
A human microbe containing divine power,
And my friends, does it not occur to you,
That harmony implicit in both macrocosm and microcosm,
Universe, human and tiniest insect,
Is explicit evidence of Godliness,
For those whose single third eye opens,

And mystic sight replaces dualistic thinking,
Is it not clear beyond any doubt,
For one who reconnects all fragments,
All dimensions, every inter-connected facet,
That universe is one living organism,
Married in spirit and perceived by soul,
Once choices are made in freedom,
That remove blinkers and dissolve obstacles,
Bringing a reawakened soul into glorious light,
Of Beloved who is humanity's original parent,
Shining as cosmic and earthly nature,
And as human freedom to choose well.

Purpose

Is there an exit from this quagmire,
A way out of the maze, once entered,
A pit so deep, with sides so steep,
That souls are lured into waking sleep,
Is there an escape beyond spiritual ideas,
Beyond lifetimes of seeking, striving,
Words alone have never liberated humanity,
Rather, words have often led to insanity,
And yet, as with a double edged knife,
Words used wisely can help bring a sincere soul,
To thresholds, that beckon with promises,
Promises of wonders, miracles, unknowable vistas,
That can be experienced with total being-ness,
Beyond words alone, beyond concepts,
And my friends, it is only then that a soul escapes,
Climbs out of pits of turmoil and despair,
Crawls out of quagmires, stumbles out of mazes,

It is crossing of the great bridge,

Becoming more than illusions of self,

Ever wrought across time and space,

Ever evolving yet losing sight of jewels,

More precious than world rulership,

Such is this quantum shift in consciousness,

Discovering treasure worth more than measure,

The grand treasure of purpose,

Feeling, knowing, intuiting, perceiving,

That universe is inherently purposeful,

Imbued with divine consciousness,

Human life, inherently imbued with divine purpose!

♦ ♦ ♦

A Godless universe is randomised hell,

Its purpose mere intellectual cleverness,

Borne from random collisions of particles,

Meaninglessly entangling without imperative,

Obeying mechanical laws of nature,

Nature itself reduced to Godlessness,

A universe here, as a blind watchmaker,

With no purpose other than making watches,

For those who blindly worship time,

Who are no more sighted than he,

Who wastes his life without knowing it,

In serving a Godless ruler who dreams a futile dream,

And if the watchmaker has influence over others,

Enslaves them, hypnotises, seduces, smothers,

We poor blind slaves, co-create soulless cultures,

Entertaining each other, in soul-destroying stupor,

Until inner rebellion marks a counter-movement,

A pendulum swing seeking intuited lost treasure,

Suddenly dragons of sloth and slumber,

Slink away from the gateway, sanctum of Holiness,

Then a turnabout refocuses, re-commits,

Allowing tentative entry into lands of hope,

Of renewed vigour, awakening interest, curiosity,

Questions arise, cascading into depth of soul,

A stirring, shaking, heart-rending, aliveness,

Sublime feelings flooding interior spaces,

Tears of gratitude, relief, soul is enlivened,

And behold, a miraculous epiphany unfolds,

Spirit eyes and ears perceive, hear praises,

Angelic praises sung in spirit-language,

For truth potently known through and through,

That Purpose is Godhead's sounding,

Resounding as enthusiasm for life, and love of art,

Sending out a purposeful dart that may pierce you too,

And set your soul afire!

♦ ♦ ♦

Again and again, some souls spin out of illusion,

And into illusion, into waking dreams, once again,

Into illusions of every type, in magician's den,

In the great hall of distorting mirrors,

Seeing in each mirror reflections of personal thoughts,

Gathered, garnered, self-made, thoughts,

Gathering into piece-meal caricatures, fleeting,

Ephemeral, insubstantial, ghostly mirages,

Yet magically believed to be real,

And my dear friends, in this mirrored palace,

We exist, even so in small rooms,

Rooms that belong to unexplored mansions,

Multi-level mansions unbeknown to souls,

Only knowing a small room or two,

As a frog living in a well, knowing not the ocean,

For let it be proclaimed with brutal honesty,

That in these tiny rooms temptations lurk,

Seductive sirens pleasing to physical senses,

Objects manifold thrust before sensuous eyes,

Rooms crammed full of tasty alluring morsels,

And a soul that spins out of illusion,

Into spiritual freedom, into translucent contentment,

Is followed by grey phantoms, waiting to re-capture again,

Hence roads to paradise are strewn with defeated souls,

Sitting by roadside way stations, itinerant wanderers,

Settling into rooms, caverns, anyplace called home,

And you ask, is there a purpose,

Here before us in a grand spectacle, an epic saga,

Is an evolutional game of hide and seek,

A cosmic game, with billions of human players,

Whence it is incumbent to conjoin, to cluster,

To explore the mansion we dwell within,

Here my dear co-seekers, is purpose magnificent!

♦ ♦ ♦

A wild bird flies freely, playing with wind drafts,

It passes a golden cage, with food galore inside,

It circles the cage, and again, moving closer,

Closer and closer to the open cage door,

Other birds fly by uninterested, but not our bird,

It falls prey to its desire, mixed with curiosity,

Destiny beckons as the bird enters the golden cage,

It succumbs, and as the cage door closes,

It frantically attempts to escape, but cannot,

In time it adapts to its new environment,

And forgets the life of freedom it once knew,

A cage no matter how beautifully decorated,

Cannot compare to belonging to the whole world,

So my friends, does our bird have purpose,

And if so, articulate what that is,

For you know both inside and outside of the cage,

Your soul-bird knows intimately both worlds,
It knows that choices made in freedom,
Determine what world is inhabited,
Again I ask, do you have a purpose,
Articulate what it is, for this is your life!

♦ ♦ ♦

Freedom and purpose form strange bed-fellows,
Add thought into the mixer, and welcome to Hubble-bubble,
Purpose belongs to Godhead, and freedom too was granted,
In freedom a separation occurred, thought could choose,
Choose to remain devoted and aligned to Godhead,
Or develop autonomously in this way or that,
Purpose now became either a servant of the most high,
Or diluted into channels of unholy thinking,
Purpose became chained to pretend Gods,
Demi-Gods whose very existence depended entirely,
On Godhead no longer acknowledged or believed in,

As streams of thoughts spawned substantial ideas,
Of its own fragmented fermentation, broiling, seething,
Compensating with focus diminished and sight myopic,
Existing for trinkets when heaven was on offer,
Freedom had reduced purpose into minuscule tributaries,
When awesome rivers and oceans were close by,
And again I ask you, what might your purpose be,
Your greatest purpose, that is your birth-right to remember,
And dear friends, can you articulate this in winged words!

♦ ♦ ♦

There is a purpose, personal yet universal,
Universal yet intimately, uniquely personal,
A core of overcoming, actually transforming,
From a worm of identified minuteness,
Into largesse of soul, worthy of human incarnation,
Worthy of a child born of spirit parent, Godhead,
Here my friends, awaits self-reflection,

That is purposeful, an evolutionary leap,
From history's tired old personal paradigm,
To quantum fields, post-modern, re-spiritualised,
A borderland, ledge, bridge, crossing,
For spiritual wayfarers of any shape or form,
Beginning with a good question or two,
Finally looking in mirrors of self-reflection,
Observing part-selves, an inner chorus,
Bickering, conspiring, manipulating, desiring,
A whole crowd in processes of habit's sway,
An internal city, an infernal metropolis,
All belonging to Millennial's story book,
Crafting without coherent memory,
Accumulating with no sense of continuity,
And yet, developing tiny microbe like identities,
That due to individuation, are fractals of One,
Here a mystical junction my friends,
A bridge like no other, awesome abyss,
To be crossed with no backward glance,
Into largesse of soul, freedom enhanced,

Free of crowds of tempting phantoms,

Of materialism rampant, seducing one's senses,

Of the blight of Ahrimanic unbridled, power lust,

Of guilt born from a million waking weaknesses,

A moment then of renewed commitment,

Staring in mirrors that reveal monsters,

Baring angry teeth and rapacious greed,

Faces distorted into vile representations,

A moment though of self-overcoming,

Discovering purpose, personal yet universal!

♦ ♦ ♦

What loads carried on our common backs,

Age old pack mules with karmic overloads,

Or beasts of burden, stressed desert camels,

Wandering far and wide, without relief,

Seeking ways to unload, unburden, be lightened,

Ignorant of layers of buried, condensed history,

Believing that identity is confined to single life spans,

Unforgiving in self-judgements, one's worst enemy,

Cruelly projecting blame without mirrored insights,

My friends, what purpose is there in a merry-go-round,
That in truth never arrives anywhere,
What merit in refusing to leave a mule of plaster,
That endlessly circles around synthetic hubs,
Cheered on by those who would have us remain children,
When we are long initiated into adulthood,
I tell you now, it is easy and difficult to step free,
Easy as a thunder clap rousing you to your senses,
Difficult as extricating body from quick sand,
Souls dwell in between heaven and hell,
Between freedom wisely navigated,
And freedom's journey into futile enslavement,
Freedom offers opportunities to soar with angels,
Or spiral down into moronic underworlds,
Where trapped souls thirst for sunlight,
I tell you true, demons can be cast aside,
Destiny re-aligned, soul to abide,
Soul's mission brought into clearer view,
That you may orient your vision with fresh vigour,

With inspired, intuited, experiential purpose!

♦ ♦ ♦

In journeys of a thousand miles,

Where does a soul begin,

What next step, how to proceed,

A question dredged from subterranean depths,

And gradually a response forms before inner sight,

Itself a question offered to contemplate,

What is the quality of this Omni-present moment,

This movement between heart-beats,

The next step is happening always,

It is accompanied by quality of consciousness,

Within which is awareness of present and presence,

It is this golden eternal moment, dear friends,

That a master-key drops into an outstretched hand,

Illuminating a journey of epic proportions,

Here the light that guides through dark spaces,

As stars light up night skies,

Stars that are equivalent to conscious awareness,

Lights that guide a journey of a thousand miles,

And whisper sacred messages along the way,

Destinations are unknown as should be,

Mysterious, belonging to concealed overlords,

Belonging to Godhead, to divine purpose,

Heart and mind need only focus on now,

Quality of here and now, a magical potential,

A next step flowing, dissolving into a river,

Steps replaced by a river of presence,

Revealing purpose as quality of being!

♦ ♦ ♦

No more stanzas spinning tales of purpose,

Move beyond, into quality of discernment,

For what quality exists at any moment,

What discernment operates, functions, guides,

If it is hazy, then know it as such,

And my friends, here the cutting edge of human life,

Here, confrontation in honest self-reflection,

Genuine contemplation, meditation, transcending time,

Transcending noisy layers of compulsive thinking,

Surrendering, renunciation, bursting a bubble,

Inviting largesse of soul to sweep into being,

Permitting discernment to sharpen into a diamond,

With clear cut facets, a prism of calm wisdom,

This, a final word regarding purpose,

An epitome, midheaven of words to breathe into,

A beautiful journey alongside a cosmic odyssey!

Timeless Moment

All time wrapped up in a timeless moment,

Self likewise, soul within creation,

You are thinker, not thought,

Doer not that which is done,

Thought and deed are waves blown by a mighty wind,

Or ripples caressed by gentle breezes,

You are witness, audience, of your own play,

Director and cast of your theatrical master-work,

Puppet-master of a puppet-show all your own,

Naturally co-created with others,

In myriads of collaborative webs,

But essentially of your choosing,

My friends, you are at the hub of the wheel,

You stand as director of your destiny,

In a timeless moment where future doesn't exist,

Save the power inherent in eternal now,

You are a point encircled by layered history,

Yet a point potentially free to think and do,

With Godhead's fresh innocence and grace,

Beyond all voices of separated ego,

Aligned to source as devoted servant,

Such is the power of this timeless moment!

Silence is a friend to pure observation,

Emptiness a portal into infinity,

An open road going where it will,

Timelessness fully embracing what is,

Ah! Sweet nectar of momentary flowering,

Universe, garden of space and stars,

Poems expressing what heart knows,

Self disappears in eternity's mystery,

Be living mystics, my dear friends,

Plunge into cosmic life, through the veil,

Through mansions of mirrored reflections,

Your own projections, outpourings,

Inward into source, out into form,

Inhalation, exhalation, in perfect balance,

Integrating innermost and outermost,

Inward into silence, out into inspired speech,

In to being no-one, out into anybody-ness,

Walking a sacred tightrope, in peaceful rhythm,

Such is the grace of this timeless moment!

♦ ♦ ♦

Engaging with everydayness, without loss,

Requires dedication, will-full intention,

Not relinquishing soul clarity, periphery for centre,

Not being drawn into seductive Hubble bubble,

And yet, not throwing babies out with bath water,

Good humour wed easily to unwavering kindness,

Authentic personality, without rigidity,

Indeed my friends, walk lightly, but stay grounded,

Be mindful, observing thoughts like passing clouds,

See in the mirror of others reflections of yourself,

And be thankful for this reflected lesson-plan,

Our biographies are intertwined, fascinatingly,

No human has three heads and six legs,

We are all close relatives, one human family,

And yet it furthers not, to lose oneself in gossip,

In trivialities, slander and projected judgements,

Nor does it do justice to human potential to sink,

Into labyrinths of hopeless depression,

Or declaiming others without sufficient insight,

Without compassion and well meaning,

Therefore a vital component of our holy mission,

Is to raise consciousness to Olympian heights,

And be saintly in auras of timeless moments!

♦ ♦ ♦

Never banish others from humanity's strivings,

No child of Godhead deserves banishment,

Do not turn your face away in disgust,

Rather seek vaster understanding and forgiveness,

Bring Godhead's channelled healing to dark places,

Move beyond victimhood, desire not revenge,

Aspire for maturity of soul, it is your birthright,

Cultivate mindful, meditative equipoise,

Transcend and transform karma, your greatest capacity,

Spirit birthed souls, and no creature alive,

Is without soul or without Spirit blessings,

No soul should be banished or perceived,

As fodder for arrogant superiority,

For illusory rights of privilege,

Therefore if banishment be justified,

Let it be for lower nature,

Let it be Luceferic addiction to sensual pleasure,

When inflated into self-serving inhumanity

Let it be Ahrimanic cold hearted power-lust,

Elitist cartels desiring control at any price,

That be banished forthwith,

My friends, this appeal is to your native self-knowing,

It is an invitation to sacrifice lesser attributes,

To awaken our common spiritual inheritance,

Our universal heritage, deepest kinship,

It is time for change, from evolutions perspective,

To collectively march into a new universalism,

Whereby individualism serves one-world harmony,

When education cultivates multi-dimensionality,

Time itself a butler in a timeless mansion!

◆ ◆ ◆

Unconsciously we sentient beings are angels,

Climbing an evolution ladder, a spirit mountain,
And I'll tell you true, we are brethren,
Joined in an impulse that is without blemish,
That connects us in mysterious synchronistic waves,
For those who can recognise, communicate heart to heart,
Without envy, competitiveness and hubris,
With echoes emanating from one divine source,
However it be described, a single impulse,
Beyond all secondary manifestations, expressions,
And here at a cross-road of magnificent proportions,
Each one who is equipped to hear the call,
Can re-evaluate, re-commit and re-establish,
Co-create a civilisation founded on Godhead's vision,
There is no other reason for cosmic unfoldment,
To this end, soul clusters must conjoin in flesh,
Tributaries must meet and form strong rivers,
Eventually pouring into inspired actions,
Into oceanic expanses, transfigured culture,
Revolutionised consciousness, Homo-Spiritus,

Take notice my friends, change is upon you,

Mystic currents are flowing into receptive hearts,

As souls experience timelessness embedded in time!

♦ ♦ ♦

Souls descend into closed vaults, modern monoliths,

Artificial, neon, consumer entrapments,

A shrinking occurs, observed by over-self,

Constrictive environs with polished tiled floors,

No open fields, only walls and doors,

Lit up signs, fixed, lifeless, announcing nothing,

Souls almost soul-less, empty vessels,

This cannot be avoided, rather engaged

dispassionately,

For each incarnated human is representative,

Of humanity, and must climb out of the abyss,

Individually and as soul-clustered friends,

Into living waters, spiritualised atmosphere,

Where everything human is transformed,

Re-calibrated, where all Mephisto's army,

Turn their faces towards Godhead,

In a torrent of ecstatic revelation and renunciation,

Finally after eons of tortured separation,

Of walking aimlessly across barren landscapes,

Chasing shadows, grasping for elusive mirages,

Surviving yet not living, biological robots,

Suddenly, a timeless moment of destiny!

♦ ♦ ♦

Words alone are as menus without food,

One must plumb depths, transcend self,

Become a divinised eye even within this body,

With inner silences so powerful,

That they can swallow all sound,

One must lose all to gain all,

Dive into an ocean of non-creation,

My dear friends, be simple,

Be as new-borns, eyes wide open,

Mystery looking back at mystery,

Do not fill in blanks with doodles,

Nor silence with mental chitter chatter,

Breathe in space and silence,

Infinity and eternity, in sweet surrender,

And if miracles happen, be outwardly unmoved,

Grist for the mill, wisdom percolating quietly,

And if tragic dramas ensue, be as a tree,

A tree caught in a wind storm,

Bending with the wind but not falling.

Allow epiphanies or theophanies to be simple remembrances,

Revelations, to be destiny moments,

Understand, nothing is happening anew,

Except consciousness has ripened,

Other than you, all else obeys natural law,

Only you in freedom can create as Demi-Gods,

But with conscious, humble adherence,

To Godhead pulsing within this timeless moment!

♦ ♦ ♦

If you are to sing and dance,

Compose music and poems, afire with mystical ardour,

Celebrate with wild enthusiasm, flaying arms,

Eyes bursting from their sockets,

Attempting to give voice to the inexpressible,

But if you are swept up in mutual or solitary holy glee,

Then my friends be mindful of traps,

Metaphor may indeed be more than metaphor,

But when metaphor becomes overly funnelled,

Into separative over literalism, esoteric branding,

When mystic eyes and ears add layers of imagery,

And hybrid blends of universal and personal,

Repeat the error of the Tower of Babel,

Whereby humans can no longer understand each other,

Universality can all to easily become dogma,

Become constrictive, condensed, a finger claiming to be a hand,

Inflated and casting all else aside as misinformed or false,

Inflated as emotional modes of favoured flavours,

Into rooms of ones own preferred iconography,

Hence rooms become severed from Godhead's mansion,

Individuality splinters off from humanity,

And settles into self-created isms or so-called truths,

With intellectual over-lays justifying and elaborating,
Newly founded philosophies with reconstituted packaging,
As timeless moments with unmoving movements,
And with sacred grace, avoiding those traps,
You may sing and dance!

♦ ♦ ♦

A fine line, narrow, knifes edge,
Gossamer thin veil, separating and joining,
Balance between dimensions delicately poised,
Pendulum swings across a spectrum,
A swing measured by its arc,
As it moves now into formlessness, now into form,
And there is a point of exquisite balance,
A void, an immeasurable null, empty, supra-consciousness,
An over-Lord, a Magi behind the screen,
Who in truth is superior to any description,
Any cosmology, esoteric philosophy, psychology,
Who as master artist is capable of producing,

Any manner of creative master-pieces,

And my friends, with this universal revelation,

All differences dissolve into respected variations,

Humanity returns to the garden, but in freedom,

In conscious unified at one-ness,

With only one authentic religion blossoming,

The supernal religion of love and wisdom,

Of unstained harmony and joy,

Then a festival of many colours,

Of multiple performances, a harmony festival,

Celebrating Godhead's omnipotent capacity,

To create in diversity, as nature too embodies,

Honour indeed your own favoured cloth,

Enjoy your living metaphor revealing Godhead,

But do not claim all knowledge, demoting others in your wake,

Do not expel others who discover truth in other forms,

Do not defend skin whilst ignoring bones,

Then a truly regal all inclusive timeless moment,

Will herald in a new age worthy of its grand title!

Again a mirror is held up, as must be,
A scribe reacting to externalities,
How can it be otherwise, as a passing parade,
Ventures past one's gaze, evoking, stirring,
Bringing to view how one is erring.
Timelessness squeezed into time capsules,
And once again a mirror, nay, a hall of mirrors,
Reflects an inner landscape, diverse, complex,
Refreshing sleep, restful silence then remind,
As images fade, reactions unwind,
A message from a spirit realm,
Meditate on 'what is', surrender, let go,
Transcend all thought, emotion, invite flow,
Calm depth encountered, peace, what is,
Time loosens its grip, allowing time to slip,
Perspective shifts as does feeling,
Spirit re-enters, gently revealing,
Ahriman has undergone revision once more,
Over reacting was a deep rooted flaw,
Bringing his power into service to Source,

The only real solution of course,

A lesson of how loops take souls out,

Away from Godhead's vision, out and about,

You fall to ground often but here is a gift,

To pick up a jewel as you consciously shift,

Then with grace by your side,

Timeless moments will abide!

♦ ♦ ♦

Think a noble thought, feel it's worth,

Bring it to the boil, then allow it to simmer,

And then dear co-creators, do something,

Sing it, write or paint it, invest your energy,

Remove barriers of doubt and fear,

Do not become overwhelmed into passive inertia,

Do not be underwhelmed into manic escapism,

Nor lose inspired ideas in forests of theoretical considerations,

Mental gymnastics, crippling procrastinations,

Here then a recipe for ailing souls,

Bent over with weighty loads,

Burdened with too many aborted attempts,
That having given birth to, never reached maturity,
First my friends, empty mind of habitual thoughts,
That are tiresome, mundane and uninspired,
Meditate as in a room with open windows,
Inviting noble thoughts to enter,
An idea sent by muses, received gratefully,
If it is spirit sent, it will warm heart and mind,
If soul imbibes it, allows it to ruminate, digest,
If soul intention permits free passage, so it can ingest,
A timeless moment arrives, a threshold, portal,
When will-full action takes up the cudgel,
Takes hold of a baton, and dares to orchestrate,
Without judgement or harsh critic spoiling,
With no defeat that would have ego recoiling,
Rather a rite of passage, liberating,
Across a bridge, manifesting, invigorating,
A song, painting, poem, whatever unfolding,
Soul has become expanded, released,
Voices limiting, thwarting have now ceased,

No karmic ghosts haunting, ridiculing, baiting,
Timeless moments, exteriorised, incarnating!

♦ ♦ ♦

This is a holy trick, your sacred task,
To integrate Godhead with persona's mask,
To be spirit, soul and ego too,
Inwardly still, outwardly do,
Fly free with grounded-ness intact,
Combining factors, unifying in fact,
Wedding for time and eternity,
Angels and humans as fraternity,
In mystical wholeness, healing balm,
Heartfelt communing, kind and calm,
Introspection forging goals ahead,
With home-coming felt instead of dread,
If world becomes a whirl and swirl,
Knowing a sanctuary where tensions unfurl,
Learning from nature's lush greenery,
Discovering new abilities amidst river and tree,
Aligning embodiment with rhythmic heart-beat,

Hearing sacred music guiding one's feet,
Being simple, wise, childlike yet grownup,
Receptive, filled with ambrosia, over-spilling one's cup,
Focused truth a protection, divine seed,
As death gives life, uprooting the weed,
Dying to time then is also a ruse,
Timeless embracing with soul's life giving muse!

Hearken...Hallelujah

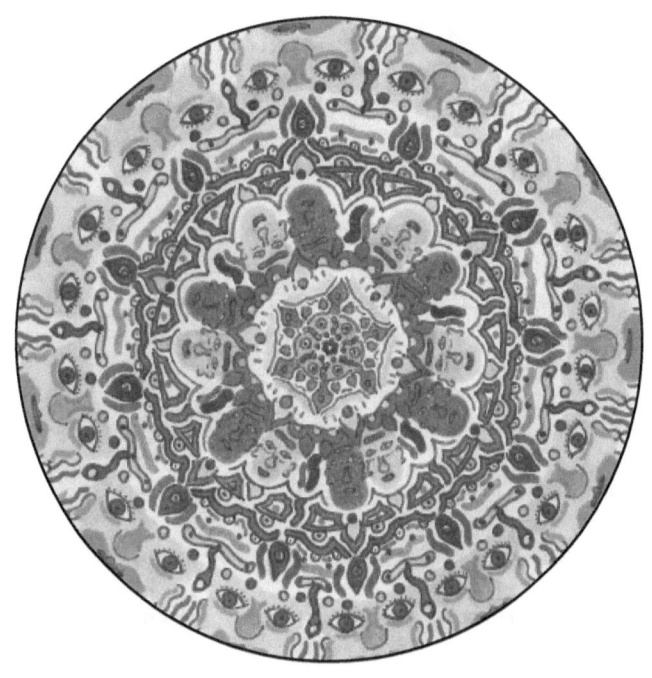

Hearken! These inspired words are only pointers,

For words can only bring you to an oasis,

You must enter and rest under its shaded trees,

Feel cool breezes wafting from lily ponds,

Words are intimations, sign posts,

Meaningful metaphors perhaps,

They suggest, imply, tease, challenge,

But beyond strings of words,

There are greater treasures by far,

And these, my friends, you must find,

By other means, experientially,

As tested self-evident truths,

With sharpened introspection,

With clear observation,

Mindfulness on foundation of emptiness,

Actual practices that stand the test of time,

Meditation, puja, burning dross,

Leaving only gold, ambrosia,

Words hinting, pointing, encouraging,

Close your eyes, invite light,

Shut your ears, invite sacred sound,
Follow breath mindfully, in and out,
Rest active tongue with its nerve endings,
Observe thoughts as sparks that live,
For a brief moment and then fade away,
Be a wedding guest at heaven's feast,
Celebrate infinity and finite betrothed,
Godhead, soul and ego hitched,
Body, mind and spirit in holy at-one-ment,
Hallelujah!

♦ ♦ ♦

Hearken! Hidden within power-terms,
A secret message,
Anthroposophy has two such occult words,
Neatly enshrouded, blanketed, mystically inserted,
Anthro and Sophy, two intimate cousins,
Hiding behind a curtain, peeking out,
To see if anyone notices them, even engages in dialogue,
Anthro, a keystone message meaning all humanity,

Sophy, a feminine cousin whose full name is Sophia,
It is she who secretly directs human evolution,
From an invisible abode behind a screen of manifestation,
She, who is as divine loving nurturer,
Appears as cosmic mother,
Sophia, Mary, Durga, Isis, Holy mother of Godhead,
Without whom humanity would have no anchor,
No resting place to lay one's head,
No way of feeling kinship with all sentient beings,
Sophia, universal beloved who sits in perfect equipoise,
Between all polarities, queen of harmony,
Wisdom bearer, eternal consort and companion,
Feel her pervasive motherly love as nectar,
Coursing through your spiritual veins,
Through your soul, into your heart and mind,
Anthro-Sophia, your very soul-beauty, love, kindness,
Surrender and invite her to be your innermost guide,
For now and evermore, Hallalujah!

♦ ♦ ♦

Hearken! Sophia stirs souls into reverence,

For brief moments transported into paradise,

New Jerusalem, archetypal Utopia,

Into heavenly abodes where angels dance,

And music of the spheres is heard,

Where human becomes more than human,

Mortality tinged by immortal nectar,

Perception transfigured by divine love,

It is closer than mind can know,

Closer than any external object,

Embedded in heart, as an implanted vision,

Of Sophia, Goddess incarnated again,

Who walks this earth unseen,

Except by those whose spirit eye has opened,

She enraptures, recaptures, souls that have thirsted,

Longed for this holy vision, to kiss her breast,

Sophia, beloved, who melts ego,

Who inspires all muses to celebrate,

To sing in a mystical chorus,

Hallelujah!

Hearken! A time nears when only life moves forth,

When all division becomes unified,

In a cosmic mystery play,

My friends, we are parts of each other,

Belonging to one theatre director,

Who surges and falls back into silence,

We are branches of one tree,

And when consciousness surrenders its accumulation,

Sacrifices its karmic load, its ingrained attachment,

Sophia then appears, within a soul emptied,

She in truth is your own Christ consort,

Your own tenderest, delicate inner flower,

She is your mother and lover,

A bride like no other,

Who once felt in deepest heart chamber,

Opens doors to worlds within worlds,

Three eyes now function in unison,

Holy trinity, holy family of humanity,

Channelled into representatives of humankind,

It is here that art must rise up,

Create metaphors, sculptures, cathedrals,
That bow low in awed reverential devotion,
It is at such destiny moments, portals into Oneness,
That evolution reaches beyond limitation,
Beyond the beyond, and yet fully incarnate,
And multi-dimensional wholeness completes the crossing.
Now, simple joyous living, a gentle voicing of,
Hallelujah!

♦ ♦ ♦

Hearken! Dreams upon dreams fade,
Layers of personal history disintegrate,
Then my dear friends, who is left,
And when shadows disappear,
Like smoke, who is bereft,
Who is here now hearing these words,
I implore you as a mirror to your soul,
Strip away what has been poured into you,
Be pure innocent consciousness,
Every time world encroaches, or identity rules,

Practice sweet renunciation, with soul knowing,

Die into Sophia's bosom, rebirth glowing,

Be reborn multiple occasions, everyday,

When clever mind becomes carried away,

With its own false light, shadows encroach,

Not sun but a mere lightbulb, invades,

Turn off, switch off and embrace darkness,

Sacred darkness, will ignite spiritual sun,

True light will illuminate and shine,

See once more, no longer blind,

When emotions flood soul with barbed arrows,

Lucifer, foaming with heated lust,

Hooking human weakness in its snare,

Retreat and inner sanctum restore,

Light of Sophia-Christ, no longer ignore,

When cold blooded reptilian Ahriman usurps,

Death knells resound, rattle and shake,

Turn about, get thee behind me,

Christ-Sophia risen, Devil will flee,

Refuse entry to this unwelcome guest,

And my dear friends, each victory,

Claimed by striving souls in our epic saga,

Acknowledged with a heart-felt intoning,

Hallelujah!

♦ ♦ ♦

Hearken! awaken, listen closely,

'Tis a book written with our blood,

Life-blood of tears and joys,

With a million, million acts of freedom,

Mutually interwoven into this kingdom,

Over innumerable eons of earthbound time,

Yet all administered by source divine,

All sparks of one great flame,

No matter how known or by what name,

A great spiralled metamorphosis in motion,

Infused by love shards bringing potion,

Yes, this poetic offering, a gift sublime,

A yearning soul as scribe transmitting,

For Godhead's ambrosia befitting,

You are fallen Angels, seeking redemption,

Then indeed fall to your knees, restore,
Redeem, recalibrate, implore,
A gateway waits you on a floor,
However deep underworlds have been,
Close by, another holy scene,
Ultimately a pledge forthcoming,
Homecoming, soul's ascension,
A final divinely inspired intention,
All dross melted leaving gold pure,
No greater blessing, no finer cure,
And with enthusiasm mustered gleefully,
Soul cluster joined in mystical chorus,
Resounding across the universe,
Hallelujah!

Glory Be!

Third eye opening, glory be!
One above duality is how to see,
Geometrical metaphor complex and simple,
Paradoxical as isolated thought alone,
But my friends, listen attentively,
A portal beckons, invites you enter,
Presented here as metaphor envisioned,
Meditate, contemplate, up and down,
Across all directions, with a central point,
Or horizontal, vertical and most high,
Geometric metaphors for your spirit-eye,
Entwined as representative of humanity,
Quality and quantity kissing, embracing,
All in all amassing, connecting, encasing,
Quantities domain, thought, feeling, will,
Qualities refrain, aligning with Godhead,

Awareness balanced, both active and still,
Across divide between Trinitarian realms,
Thinking clear, inspired by Christ-Sophia,
Feeling, potently with surrendered heart,
Willing, embodying in focused intention,
A trinity emblazoned by Light supreme,
Sacred pledge re-engendered, re-wrought,
Greatest battle engaged with and fought,
Defeating Mephisto's double pointed spear,
Ancient pact was made, Lucifer with self,
Then with out-growth, Ahriman's stealth,
Until trinities dedication to Godhead's vision,
Pledge unequaled among human-kind,
Nearing, closing to ascension's grace,
Harmonising two sides of a human face,
Quality and quantity with a supra element,
An overseer, your personalised soul,
Re-imagining divinity's omniscient goal,
Godhead, individuated yet universal,
Chorus Mystica, all-splendour, gained,

Flying into spheres freely attained,

Glory be to the most high,

Glorious opening of your third eye!

♦ ♦ ♦

Glory be! A single wondrous eye opens,

And all is seen with crystalline clarity,

A single ear hears with calmest depth,

Breath becomes as omnipotent unity,

All worlds mesh, meld, harmonise,

Inter-weave as symphonic masterwork,

You are such as microcosm, dear friends,

Also secretly macrocosm in your finer attire,

How can you open this mystical door,

How to embrace your full identity,

As creator and creature entwined,

As thinker and thought aligned,

Doer and done, in rhythmic tandem,

And who is this creator, thinker, doer,

Who are you, witness of all, conscious observer,

Even observer of yourself, as in a mirror,

Are you acquainted with Christ-Sophia,

With Godhead and universal Selfhood,

With a single eye that towers over everything,

And yet partakes in every momentary drama,

Have you awakened to primordial being,

Known by multitudes of names, symbols,

And yet a divine singularity, without shadow,

Can you be someone and no-one simultaneously,

In and out of time-space with equanimity,

My dear friend, you are universe and molecule,

Beyond every separation unity prevails,

One interwoven matrix, web of life,

You only need to peek behind the screen,

Only need to see beyond what is seen,

Glory be to the sacred marriage,

Wed by glorious overseer, of third eye!

✦ ✦ ✦

Life begets life, glory be!

Whether incarnate or discarnate, life is,

You and life, two peas in a pod,

Consciousness eternal, brightly or dim,
Need not be capricious, nor by whim,
I am is everyone, every living being,
Rayed out, hence individuated seeing.
Pure disembodied consciousness,
By greatest Creator's magic will,
Suddenly existing among countless others,
As branches, leaves and fruit on one tree,
You, who are presence pure, deep, omnipotent,
A tree fully laden, complete, replete,
Ah, my dear friends, penetrate, explicate,
Revelation is upon waters of oceanic being.
Truly, you are not of this world alone,
A cosmic traveller are you wearing stardust,
Constituted of Stella light, alchemically condensed,
Energy vibrations, frequencies waving, pulsating,
Miracle of life, miracle of you,
Cosmic work of miraculous art,
And here in earthly grandeur, nature's bounty,
Here too incarnated human, Godhead's handiwork,

With inner invisible seed, of potential spiritual awakening,
A threshold unequaled in terrestrial evolution,
Open that third eye, ear and heart chamber,
Break through misty sensual captivity,
Proclaim with trembling ecstasy,
Glory be most lofty of human endeavours,
One unified field of living beings,
Homo-Spiritus, seed become tree bearing fruit!

♦ ♦ ♦

Metaphors aside, you are a single eye,
Observing as one conscious seer,
A physically hidden eye, yet self-evident,
And if you sink calmly into this eye,
You will encounter a mysterious ocean,
An ocean without boundaries,
With no waves or ripples,
No disturbance, agitation or madness,
Here my friends, you will meet yourself,
A mysterious self, unlimited, infinite,

From here, a vantage to observe,

All as in a passing parade,

Then eye meets heart, hence love bursts forth,

As a deliciously scented flower blossoming,

Knowing it's time has arrived,

A culminating moment, love streams out,

Love is understood by love,

Singular heart-eye lovingly rejoices,

Spreading warmth to cold environs,

And coolness to arid overly hot zones,

Eye of love, dwelling within,

Glory be to thee,

You who are mother, father,

And glorified love-child,

Cosmic eye incarnated as your loving blessing!

❖ ❖ ❖

What a challenge it is, oh great eye,

To integrate two with one, three aligned,

To infiltrate two, from one's domain,

Three-pronged merger, magical trinity,

Glory be as devotion to infinity,

And yet dear friends, listen close,

A mighty challenge is near at hand,

For single wakened eye is not enough,

As light must shine on something real,

Sun and moon need to compliment,

All dimensions must coalesce,

Must contribute harmoniously,

That which is far is close,

That which is close is far,

Together they present archetypes of each other,

Parallel realities, archetypal patterns,

Hence opening a great single eye,

Is human and Godly both,

Just as two eyes of separation,

Both heavenly and earthly are,

As stone and distant star,

What a challenge, for one great eye,

To be recognised by two who see double,

Twins must transcend duality,

This my friends, is the true incarnation,

Of singularity, Godhead, I Am,

Revered first by Sophia-Christ,

Followed by Homo-Spiritus,

This is the second coming.

When human consciousness will rise up,

And proclaim: Glory be to the most high!

✦ ✦ ✦

Glory be for the opening of the third eye,

And hence down-flow of eternal light,

As those of old worshipped Ra,

Supernal sun of which all stars receive brilliance,

Bringing life to our magnificent cosmos,

Permeated by Godhead's loving grace,

Ain Soph, boundless light, glory to thee,

Sitting above all creation, mystery of mysteries,

Holiest of holies, universal consciousness,

Flowing into wakened eye,

An eye that looks up and down,

Up to heavens, down to earth,

One single split eye, vertical in nature,
Capable of vertically joining heaven and earth,
In a unified multi-cosmos,
This microcosmic multi-verse as poetic offering,
Humble terrestrial eye barely opened,
And yet, a crack letting light in, inviting,
Birthing another phase of sacred evolutional sighting.
Oh glory be to this human potential,
Omnipresently sleeping, waiting for dawn,
Waiting for great eye to creatively spawn,
Wonders unheralded by Maya's web,
Wave of a magic wand over eyes closed tight,
Could bring daylight into unconscious night,
See all as dream images, mere paint strokes,
Colours, tones, that Godhead invokes,
Transcend yourself, knowingly, free,
Your prayerful gratitude, glory be!

♦ ♦ ♦

Can another word be uttered now,
Endless language would surely fail,

Emptiness must exist if fullness be,
As underground seed contains fullest tree,
A never ending story, if truth be told,
Mystery pure, alchemists gold,
Pure awareness omnipresently now,
Paradoxically, stories end can entail,
Yin and yang with Tao above,
Tao pulsing everlasting love,
Sophia, Christ as wedded pair,
Godhead, Source, Mystery fair,
Mind that intellectualises, logics redress,
Minor script that must sincerely confess,
Bubble believing it is gigantic sphere,
Must burst asunder, then Source can steer,
So words fade gradually quiet,
Dissolving, melting, sweet surrender,
Primal tone and light remaining,
Deep rest, beyond discursive naming,
Silence embraced, enshrined, accepted,
Engulfed by cosmic radiance reflected,

Meditative in-turning, portal ajar,

Outermost floods into core from afar,

An epic poem gifted from heart,

Glory be that we are never apart,

Hearken, Single Eye, Hallelujah, Freedom,

All has been spoken, Aum, Aum, Aum!

Epilogue

Ascension, last act, immanent,
Magic moment waited for,
Quantum leap, heaven sent,
Crossing to Shambala's shore,
Only one choice left to make,
At journey's end, final round,
Only one thirst left to slake,
For every show is time-bound,
Every future, hope laden, desire,
Each pursuing tomorrow's dream,
History's multifarious conspire,
Blocked from oceans, polluted stream,
Dammed by hollow spaces,

Untapped, unseen timeless places,

Godhead omnipresently hidden,

Would reveal if only bidden,

Has never been another tale,

Never, cosmic impulse varied,

Merely relative different scale,

Ascension's muses simply buried,

Evolution, mighty story-line,

Has led to threshold's sacred cliff,

Words melding beyond sublime,

Into Sophia's arms, only if,

And yet my dear dear friends, Hearken,

An epic is not shared in vain,

For a journey embarked hand in hand,

Transformed more than we can explain,

You are more by far than words can tell,

More than poets and scribes can show,

Deeper than the deepest well,

Stronger than the strongest flow,

One moment pledged earnestly,

Knowing incarnation intimately,
One dedicated will-full pledge, on the level,
Overcoming compromises with the devil,
An age old pact relinquished true,
Sacrificing traumatised compensations too,
Final choice of pledge over pact,
Unified, harmonious embodiment intact,
You are Godhead, Christ and she,
Sophia, Cosmic mother, bride to be,
You are macrocosm in full display,
Microcosm, as Creation's way,
My soul friend I'll wait for you,
Likewise, we shall wait for others too,
Ascending, as wild flowers in a field,
Where nothing toxic to desire or build,
Then secret, mystery, Godhead's vision,
Known, felt, perceived, end of revision,
All dimensions merged, peace will bring,
Concluding chorus, hallelujah, we shall sing!

www.ingramcontent.com/pod-product-compliance
Lightning Source LLC
Chambersburg PA
CBHW020657300426
44112CB00007B/414